My Dog, My Guru

A Dog's Principles for a Happier Life

Gilles Moutounet

HAY HOUSE

Carlsbad, California • New York City • L
Sydney •Johannesburg • Vancouver • Ne

Published and distributed in the United Kingdom by:
Hay House UK Ltd, Astley House,
33 Notting Hill Gate, London W11 3JQ
Tel: +44 (0)20 3675 2450; Fax: +44 (0)20 3675 2451
www.hayhouse.co.uk

Published and distributed in the United States of America by:
Hay House Inc., PO Box 5100, Carlsbad, CA 92018-5100
Tel: (1) 760 431 7695 or (800) 654 5126
Fax: (1) 760 431 6948 or (800) 650 5115
www.hayhouse.com

Published and distributed in Australia by:
Hay House Australia Ltd, 18/36 Ralph St, Alexandria NSW 2015
Tel: (61) 2 9669 4299; Fax: (61) 2 9669 4144
www.hayhouse.com.au

Published and distributed in the Republic of South Africa by:
Hay House SA (Pty) Ltd, PO Box 990, Witkoppen 2068
info@hayhouse.co.za; www.hayhouse.co.za

Distributed in Canada by:
Raincoast Books, 2440 Viking Way, Richmond, B.C. V6V 1N2
Tel: (1) 604 448 7100; Fax: (1) 604 270 7161; www.raincoast.com

Text © Gilles Moutounet, 2017

A catalogue record for this book is available from the British Library.

ISBN: 978-1-78180-932-7

Photography © Gilles Moutounet; illustration © Bob Stokes

To all the mistreated dogs: I hope that one day, people will see the guru within you.

To mum: who would have been happy to hold this book.

To dad: hoping that you will be able to read this book one day. It would mean that you had worked on your English or that the book has found a French editor. :-)

To Skottï: for sharing his wisdom with me.

Contents

Prelude

As a kid, I wasn't fond of dogs – or rather, I was just indifferent to them. At our home in Paris, France (where I spent my childhood), we didn't have pets, so perhaps that was the reason. However, it's no secret that exposure and experiences in life can make you change your mind dramatically.

For me, dogs were animals that barked for no reason, put their noses in dirty places, and left their poop on pavements without a care in the world. (The latter is extremely annoying, although, according to an old French superstition, it's a sign of good luck when you step in it with your left shoe. However, I always thought this must have been intended as a consolation prize for the unfortunate person affected.)

Like many kids, I enjoyed teasing dogs once in a while. During one such incident, when I was around 11 years old, I was on my way to church to attend my weekly religious education class when I met a dog on the street. He was sat outside a supermarket waiting for his owner, but he took an interest in me and starting following me. Amused, I pretended to have food in my hand and made him continue for quite some distance.

Of course, I was too young and stupid to worry, or even care, about how the dog would find his way back. I wasn't thinking about the owner either, who may have panicked when he discovered his pet had gone missing.

I just left the dog in the middle of nowhere and ran away. Ironically, I was going to church to learn good principles in life; I'm not sure I was ready to apply them at that age. As can be concluded from this story, I wasn't much interested in dogs or their wellbeing. Neither was I much interested in church!

Today, Paris is but a distant memory as I have since settled in India with my family. Six years ago, my wife decided to get a dog as a gift for our two daughters, but I was strongly against the idea. In fact, I tried to convince her that having a dog in the house would be *such* a nuisance.

'Who will take care of him?' I asked. 'Who will toilet train him?' 'What will we do with him when we fly out for our annual holiday?' I tried my very best to dissuade her, but as always, where there's a will there's a way. A dog they wanted and a dog they got! And they named him Skottï.

I couldn't possibly have imagined then that, six years down the line, I would write a book inspired by the new member of our family. I'd like to take this opportunity to thank Skottï – our faithful springer spaniel – for being such a gentle companion, and so full of love and happiness; as you'll see, he certainly knows how to live a happy life.

I hope that you enjoy reading this book as much as I enjoyed writing it.

Happy reading!

~

Introduction

Anyone who's had the privilege of owning a dog must have, at least once, envied its life and its happiness.

A dog is always at the door to welcome you when you arrive home – no matter what – wagging his tail with pure happiness. Whether you're returning from a week-long holiday or a five-minute trip to the postbox, a dog's excitement level remains the same. He often barks as if you'd left not less than a year ago, and jumps up at you, even if your hands are loaded with shopping bags.

Well, I must have envied my dog's life close to 10,000 times. One day, as this faithful creature sat at my feet, looking at me with sympathy in his eyes, I started reflecting on *how* and *why* he always seems so happy; how and why he's never hassled by anything, and overall, is perfectly content with his life!

I thought to myself: 'Is there any chance I could learn something from him, in order to change *my* life for the better? Or at least change my *attitude* toward life in general?'

After all, Albert Einstein had encouraged us to do just that when he said, 'Look deep into nature, and then you will understand everything better.' Einstein was a genius and a great thinker – his theory of relativity led to new ways of looking at time, space, matter, energy and gravity. This assertion that nature can be our teacher, and that it has answers to all our questions, was wisdom that had helped him in his own work.

In fact, the idea that nature is our teacher has been shared throughout human history. For example, in the Bible it says:

> *'But ask the beasts, and they will teach you;*
> *the birds of the heavens, and they will tell you;*
> *or the bushes of the earth, and they will teach you;*
> *and the fish of the sea will declare to you.'*
> Job 12:7–8

I haven't included this quote to add a religious angle to what I have to say. By quoting Einstein (who was Jewish) along with the Bible, I'm highlighting the fact that wisdom has a universality that goes beyond religious faith. (Quoting from the Bible also reassures me that attending those religious classes when I was a kid wasn't a total waste of time, as I once believed!)

Coming back to nature, it's also universally recognized and accepted that mankind has never invented anything. Everything was already here – existing in nature – and we've only observed and imitated what nature has created on its own. A perfect illustration of this principle is the zip. Invented in 1851 by American Elias Howe, its design was directly inspired by birds' feathers, which have interlocking barbs along their length. Needless to say, there are countless other examples that have proven this principle, time and again.

Thus, with the support of the eminent A. Einstein and a bestselling book called the Bible, I decided to look deep into my dog's eyes and start a one-to-one interaction with him. My aim was to see how he could inspire my daily life. If I could get answers to my questions, perhaps in turn, I'd gain some wisdom.

All dog owners must have heard other dog owners say something along the lines of, 'Oh, these precious animals have so many things to teach us!' – without being too specific about *what* exactly those things are. Yes, I know they are broadly talking about the 'unconditional love' that these four-legged pets give to their owners, but is there more to it? Nature was definitely enticing me to find out all I could from it.

Skottï certainly had a good, simple, happy life and, after observing him for many hours, I realized that he seemed to have acquired the perfect balance in life that we humans work so hard to achieve. This couldn't be down to all the self-help books that *I* had bought on the subject, unless he was reading them behind my back!

No, for Skottï, it seemed to be much simpler. It was as if all this wisdom was inbuilt in his nature – available to him in the blink of an eye – as opposed to my striving with long and tiresome reading sessions.

One day, I suddenly realized that Skottï was *more* than a dog. Perhaps it's because we live in India, which is renowned as the land of the mystical and the spiritual, but after observing Skottï over a long period, I came to see that he resembles a monk in a Tibetan monastery: always quiet (except when the bell rings, I have to admit) and always content with life.

From then on, I decided to look at him from another perspective – as a guru – and I resolved to try and record his wisest principles. After all, the word 'dog' is an anagram of 'God', so there could definitely be a connection. Moreover, I'd never really believed in God, and in this way, I might get close to it, to see where it would take me!

So, after several long conversations with my four-legged guru – and with the help of a wee bit of imagination – I came up with a few simple rules that, if respected on a daily basis, can be of great help to anyone wanting to live a happier life.

'Hmmm …' I guess that's what most of you must be thinking at this point, but don't worry, I won't be suggesting that you live like a dog. I won't be asking you to greet people by sniffing their bum! Instead, I'll be asking you to observe eleven basic principles, set by our guru, that are also the gist of everything I talk about in this book:

- Trust and have faith in the master
- Live in the now
- Be grateful and express gratitude
- Communicate better
- Practise unconditional love
- Play with nature
- Improve the way you relate to others
- Be patient
- Use your intuition
- Beware of Pavlovian conditioning
- Do yoga: the dog poses

~

Chapter 1

Trust and have faith in the master

When Skottï was still a puppy, we returned home one evening after a day out and didn't receive our usual super-excited, manic greeting from him. In fact, he was lying calmly on the floor, looking at us with a sad expression.

We discovered that Skottï had developed a serious inflammation on his head and mouth, and as a result, was very uncomfortable. He was having difficulty breathing and, when he saw his family looking so worried, he became a bit panicky, wondering what was happening to him.

We tried to figure out what had caused the inflammation. Was it a bug bite? Was it a food allergy? We called the vet out immediately, even though it was late at night.

However, after spending just a few minutes with us, Skottï seemed more at ease. The fact that he was no longer alone, and that his masters had returned (even though we had no idea how to help him feel better), appeared to be a big relief. The moment we entered the house, things started looking up for him. He must have been in a lot of pain, but his eyes began to shine when he saw us, and his spirits lifted.

What was the reason for this sudden change in him? It was simple: the master was back home, and he had complete faith that the master would know how to fix what was happening to him. It's true that Skottï is always happy when we're around – this four-legged soul creature never seems to worry about anything.

Do you imagine Skottï actually thinks about where his next meal is coming from? Is he concerned that he might not have that comfortable bed to sleep in at night? Does he spend hours wishfully wondering whether he'll have an outing or a walk the following day? Or even a special treat for his birthday?

Not at all! He doesn't care about any of this. Because it's not his concern – *it's his master's*.

Rest assured, there will always be food for him and a place to sleep. He'll also get a special treat for his birthday (which, to be honest, makes the owner of the local pet store much happier than the birthday boy himself).

But, coming back to the point, is this the secret of Skottï's eternal happiness? Well, if we start taking notes from nature, it's a good lead. After this incident, I started to wonder what it would be like if I were a dog. What would this mean for me?

During my early life, I wasn't fond of religion and considered myself an atheist, more or less, even though I came from a Catholic background. In fact, religious people – especially the orthodox ones who pretend to follow their faith and its principles to the letter – didn't appeal to me, regardless of what religion they followed.

I always found all the 'rules' inherent in organized religion limiting. I could never understand why not eating a particular thing or praying in a particular manner would make someone better in the eyes of God (if there was one).

Maybe it was down to the manner in which I was introduced to religion; we shall never know. But, in the Old Testament – which is the part of the Bible kids learn about first – God appears to be a very strong character and is highly authoritarian.

In the story of Adam and Eve, in which the original sin is introduced with the notion of 'good' and 'bad', God seems particularly strict; he's not someone you'd like to have to deal with every day. From the Old Testament, I got the understanding that there were big differences between people, and that some go to heaven while others go to hell; that's also the message I got from other religions, too.

Such big and scary concepts can frighten any kid, and push them away from religion rather than closer to it. Many years had passed since then, but I wasn't sure if I was ready to introduce the concept of 'God', or some higher master, to take care of my needs.

That was, until I read books by Robin Sharma, Deepak Chopra and Neale Donald Walsch, among others. These writers don't speak of religion per se, but about happiness and life principles. I don't know whether they are in the same league as Muhammad, Jesus or the Buddha, but to me, they are good prophets in their own way because their message and purpose is clear, simple and well explained.

They all agree that there's something above and beyond us; we could call it God if we wanted to, but also a higher intelligence, energy, master, or simply the universe. This way of thinking certainly appealed to me the most. I admit that it changed my perception and managed to reintroduce the concept of 'God' into my life.

This awakening – if I may call it that – convinced me that I should research and learn more about the subject. Eventually, it helped me draw a parallel between the relationship that dogs have with their owner or master, and the relationship that some human beings have with a higher dimension – one we could also call master – the universe, higher power or energy… even life itself.

According to this association of thoughts and parallelism, if a dog has a master to look after him, human beings have one too! The only difference is that Skotti can see me, come over and lick my cheek if he wants to, and knows when I'm around, whereas we don't have the same capacity to see or feel our own master – at least not physically.

But we consider ourselves superior to animals because have the ability to think of abstract ideas, while animals cannot. We have the ability to think of concepts, ideas and other intangible things.

So, if we accept the existence of this master, which can be extremely challenging at times, it's only the beginning of what nature has to teach us. In fact, it's telling us that we need to trust our master and have faith! It's that simple.

When Skottï was in a bad shape that day and wondering what was happening to him, he was rejuvenated by his faith in us. This means a lot, and many people have already recognized this phenomenon. In her book *The Law of Attraction*, Deborah Morrison says that 'we need to turn our worries about money, food, shelter and the future to a higher power.'

Another powerful statement along the same lines can be found in Annemarie Postma's book, *The Deeper Secret*. She says that 'when we do let go of what is most important to us, the universe takes care of things well.'

As you've hopefully clearly understood, the main idea here is just to let go of those things. In fact, we should even be *inclined* to do so, as this idea is shared by different faiths and is universal in its approach.

While I've quoted here from contemporary books on the subject, it should be noted that the same sentiment appears in both the Bible and the Koran:

> 'Therefore do not be anxious, saying, "What shall we eat?" or "What shall we drink?" or "What shall we wear?" For the Gentiles seek after all these things, and your heavenly Father knows that you need them all. But seek first the kingdom of God and his righteousness, and all these things will be added to you.'
>
> MATTHEW 6:31–33

> 'What is with Allah is better than diversion and than a transaction, and Allah is the best of providers.'
>
> SURAH AL-JUMU'AH: 11

This simple principle is clearly followed by Guru Skottï. The guru doesn't think of his next meal because, somehow, he knows that his master will take care of it. And that's what I call having faith!

At our level, this means that we shouldn't worry, but instead trust the universe to take care of it. It also means that the master knows what's best for us and tells us everything we need to know. In the same way, the dog will never question the need for that trip to the vet – he will go, led by his master, because the master is doing it for his benefit!

That's fantastic news. Our God, higher power or universe – you can even call it your angels – is there for us all the time, taking care of all our needs!

This also means that we should drop all expectations in life. As human beings, we tend to think we know what's best for us. We try to plan our lives and have a great many expectations with regard to relationships, career path, status and so on. Most of the time, those expectations lead to frustration and resentment, making them counterproductive to living a happy life.

What nature is telling us is that there's no need to do this. Our job is only to trust nature; to believe that the masters know what they are doing; to know that whatever life throws at us, it's always for our own good; and that we should enjoy life as much as possible. It's important that we accept whatever comes our way — be it a good meal, an outing in the park, or a trip to the vet.

Finally, this reminds me of a phrase that's quoted all over the Internet: 'Let go and let God.' If we play with those letters for the purpose of this book, we can alter the phrase to read: 'Be dog, let go, and let God.'

~

Chapter 2

Live in the now

As we now know from the first principle, Skottï always trusts us to meet his daily needs, which means he can enjoy his day without tension or worry. But that's not *it*. Skottï lives only in the present — in the now — as he has no reference to the past and doesn't have the ability to think of tomorrow.

Of course, he remembers little things he's learned in the past: for instance, he knows where his favourite treats are kept in the house and he can find his way back home. But that doesn't affect his psyche and his ability to enjoy the moment. Whether he's eating his lunch or chasing a bird on his morning walk, Skottï lives only for the present moment.

Once in a while, when he's had too much to eat, he'll have a stomach ache and, in extreme cases, even puke. He always gives us a sign when this is about to happen. Usually there are a few seconds between the signal and when he actually throws up, which gives us enough time to run into the kitchen and grab an old newspaper, which is then placed in front of him so he can do what he needs to do.

But what has always surprised me is how quickly Skottï recovers right afterwards. Once the job is done, you'll find him jumping around, happy with himself and wagging his tail — the first sign that shows the world how happy he is! It's as if nothing has happened.

On the contrary, I've been car sick many times in my life (especially when my wife is driving — okay, I'm just kidding, *wink*) and it always takes hours for me to recover from it. As a child, I would end up in my mother's arms in a bid to ease the feeling — it was as if something really monstrous had happened. Later, instead of forgetting all about it, I would wallow in self-pity! This need to feel sorry for myself didn't really help anyone — I was just adding a bit of drama to the whole experience.

Now, after reviewing the way Skottï handles his life, that clearly makes sense. Here's a good lesson or inspiration to take: we should try to live in the now as much as possible. To live in the present moment implies two other things:

1. We don't think of the past.

2. We don't think of the future.

The concept of 'living in the now for a happier life' is not new and many have focused on its importance. If we look closer at the way our mind works, we'll see that it tends to be time-bound – it's either looking at the past or at the future.

By looking at the past, we bring to our present, emotions such as regret, guilt and sadness. We go back along our memory lane and come up in the present with those memories that immediately interfere with our present feelings and manage to bring us down. At the other end of the spectrum is thinking of the future, which usually means constantly wondering what's going to happen next, either with big expectations or with worries and concerns. Again, those thoughts bring stress and anxiety to our present moment.

In *The Power of Now*, Eckhart Tolle demonstrates that he has clearly understood this phenomenon, and he expresses it so well that I highly recommend this book for future reading. Paulo Coelho, in his bestselling book *The Alchemist*, reminds us that 'if you can concentrate on the present you will be happy' as 'the secret is here in the present'.

Coelho himself might have been inspired by the Buddha, to whom the following quote is attributed: 'Do not dwell in the past, do not dream of the future, concentrate the mind on the present moment.'

These examples show us the universality of the idea of living in the now. It's the most interesting 'rule' for achieving a better life; nevertheless, it's also the most challenging, as our mind is always pondering something or other, but difficult doesn't mean impossible. In the end, the idea is to be inspired and try our best. We may not find it possible to live in the now 24/7 – in fact, I believe that few people can achieve that – but several minutes a day could be a good start.

Of course, the principle of living in the now may be even more challenging if there's nothing great happening in your life at the moment; you may find that this is a good reason to go back and visit the past or become lost in the possibility of better days hidden in the future. This temptation seems natural, but it cannot help us in the now. Instead, you can concentrate on what could make your today better, and spend all your time and effort achieving your best possible life.

～

Chapter 3

Be grateful and express gratitude

The third principle is being happy with what we have and not forgetting to express it – but what does that mean?

Skottï never misses an opportunity to show us that he's happy about something. It can be about his last meal, a visitor to our home – always a big event in a dog's life – or when we play with a ball or are involved in a similar activity. He shows his happiness and gratitude for these things, and he's able to do so because he's attached to the *present moment*, rather than to the past or to future activities.

At our level, this means we shouldn't dwell on what we had in the past or what we hope to have in the future. For example, imagine that you once had a lot more money or a great relationship that no longer exists. For whatever reason, you may have lost your fortune or your dear one, but clinging on to them in the present moment won't bring them back; instead, it will only invite sadness into your life.

In the same way, if you only think about the future – the next job, the next car or your next ideal relationship – you won't be able to concentrate on the present. The present is what exists *today* and it's where you should focus your attention! The present moment is what you have now and *nothing else*. The rest is pure illusion and irrelevant to your present condition.

But there's more to it than that. As well as being grateful for whatever you have now, you also need to *show* it. My Skottï always displays his happiness by jumping around and wagging his tail. As extraordinary as it may sound, this has a secondary benefit and advantage: in displaying his happiness in front of us, Skottï *keeps us happy*!

Of course, this doesn't apply to every situation but somehow, having a dog next to me who expresses his gratitude and happiness tends to make me happy too! In return, I do my best to make him even happier! But, as we discussed at the beginning of this book, I'm Skottï's master. We could say that I'm his world; I'm like God to him! (Hold on, there's a reason why I'm making such a strong statement.)

If I accept the theory that there's something above me – an energy, my own universe, some angels or even God – by displaying gratitude and happiness for what I have, there's a chance that my God or higher power will be happy about it, and this will earn me extra brownie points!

As extraordinary as this sounds, it's exactly what's happening. Some call it the law of attraction, but the fact remains that happiness attracts happiness. In defending this theory, many also speak of the 'vibrational state' of everything. The idea that, in life, you'll often only attract things that are in the same vibrational state as you.

When Skottï wags his tail because he's happy about his life in the moment, he's strongly sending positive vibes around him that make *me* feel happy too. This works for me more readily after a bad day at work! Think about it. You return home in a foul mood, but your dog doesn't know that you had a bad day. For him, it's business as usual.

You've just come back to him after a long day out. How nice is that for the dog!?

The dog is so grateful for that moment: he barks, jumps, wags his tail and is absolutely thrilled to see you. That's where the miracle happens. His happiness is communicative. Somehow, his good mood influences you and puts a smile on your face. You tend to feel lighter when you see so much joy around you and may even reward your dog for this.

At our level, this principle means that if we act and show happiness to the world and the universe, the universe and our own master will also shower positivity and happiness on us. It's really as simple as that. But, again, this is no more than the law of nature. If nature works like this for Skottï, why shouldn't it work that way for us?

On the same note, have you ever wondered how a dog's happiness is so well expressed through the movement of its tail? The energy within a wagging tail is very strong. So strong, in fact, that you'd better remove any glasses, vases or chinaware at its height, or you may end up with a big disaster.

This demonstrates how a *feeling* is directly translated into a physical *activity*. For the tail to wag, there has to be some internal vibration in the nervous system involving synapses and muscles. This proves that, in nature, everything is interconnected and that everything is expressed through a more or less strong vibration.

You'll find there are many ways to express gratitude. The easiest is simply to say 'thanks' to life, God or the angels, as often as possible. The idea, as you may have gathered, is not to complain about anything, but instead, try to be positive at all times. You can also jump around and dance to your favourite songs. This will immediately raise your energy levels and align you with other energies related to your own sense of happiness.

In the Koran, the Prophet rightly says:

> *'If you are grateful, I will give you more.'*
> SOORAH IBRAHIM | VERSE 7

~

Chapter 4

Communicate better

Happiness is all about communication.

Skottï may not have the ability to speak, but he *does* know how to express himself without concealing anything. How many times does Skottï need to bark in order to get our attention? Be it for food or an outing, he always knows how to express himself in the right way. He's never shy at those times.

When he's happy, he shows it; when he's upset, he shows that too and whenever he wants something, he'll communicate that effectively. Does he care if it's Sunday morning and you want to lie in for an extra hour before getting up and giving him his food? NO! He'll still come and ask for it. He's always straightforward – any time, any day!

For Skottï, communication is simple and clear, and without hidden meanings. We don't need to know how to read between the lines. This is yet another lesson on the way nature functions. We have a few things to learn with regard to communication and shouldn't assume that, as superior beings, we know it all.

As a matter of fact, communication between human beings is highly complex. For example, sometimes there are things you *want* to say but don't because you find reasons *not* to say them, such as:

- 'I'm too shy.'
- 'What will the other person think?'
- 'It's not the right time.'

The excuses are endless!

Or you'll say things that you later regret, prompting comments like:

- 'I shouldn't have said that.'
- 'I should have waited!'

On some occasions, people exaggerate when they talk, saying things that aren't necessarily correct. Sometimes there are good intentions behind the way people talk and sometimes there are bad ones – we often hear of people being called liars, manipulators, crooks...

I guess that's the main difference between human beings and other creatures: our ego is here to somehow change the communication flow and complicate it in many ways. Of course, the idea is not to pretend that we don't have an ego – obviously that's not possible, as it's just the way we humans are – but being aware of when our ego is taking over, and acknowledging it, is a way of resolving the issue.

The idea isn't to suppress the ego, then, but to cool it down and tame it. If we can train a dog, perhaps there's a way to do that to the ego! Put your mind to the job. Maybe it could be interesting to reconsider the way you communicate – to try avoiding lying and just say what you feel. This small step can be very useful.

Now that we understand the importance of communication, it really seems simpler to just take an idea forward, instead of imagining what could be going on in the other person's mind. But the way that you express yourself while taking this into account is something else to consider.

The following idea may sound basic; in fact, it's so fundamental that we may have forgotten about it. *Just speak out loud and ask for what you want!* When my family sit down for dinner with a nice chicken marinated in mustard and cream gravy, you can be sure that Skottï will soon join us and try to get a taste – even if he's already had his own dinner.

He'll declare his wish loud and clear with a straight 'Woof! Woof! Woof!' – which, translated into human language, means: 'I want some of your chicken!'

More 'Woof! Woof! Woof!' – 'Can you hear me, or shall I repeat?'

When I was a teenager, I'd discuss with my school friends ways of flirting with girls, trying to get some good advice. I had two major concerns that haunted many of my nights: the first was how to ask a girl to go out with me. To me, this seemed to be the most difficult and challenging thing I could ask of a girl. The second concern – the one most tricky to execute – would be asking permission for a kiss, but this assumed that stage one had been successfully completed!

Each of my friends had his own flirtation methods, but I got even more confused when one remarked that, for girls, communication was different and that 'yes' meant 'no' and 'no' meant 'yes'. Of course, depending on the circumstances, 'yes' could also mean 'yes' and 'no', 'no'! Basically, asking a girl out seemed to be a very tricky exercise and this advice definitely delayed my first attempt at it.

Today, playing with Skottï and asking him to bring back the ball seems so much easier in comparison. 'Bring back the ball' means 'bring back the ball'. Simple. And, for Skottï, 'I want some of your chicken' means the same. Our communication is crystal clear.

The main point I'm trying to make here is that we should just ask for what we want – while taking into consideration another parallel basic rule, which is that if you don't ask for something, you'll never get it! The same way that Skottï won't get an extra piece of chicken if he doesn't manifest himself during dinner; the same way I must have missed out on a few dates as a teenager – more from not asking than from getting a negative response.

So, now that we know the full benefits of just asking – instead of making assumptions, thinking and hoping that the other person will read our mind and guess what we want – let us not forget that this principle can be applied on a larger canvas, too.

If we return to the second principle – which asserts that if a dog has a master, so do we – this means we should ask our own master and the universe *for what we want*! Be it a job, a relationship, a healthy life… It can be anything, really. As many philosophers have put it so well: just ask and the universe (the master) will conspire to get it for you.

This principle is widespread in literature, too, starting with the Bible, of course, where we can read:

> *'And whatever you ask in prayer, you will receive, if you have faith'.*
>
> MATTHEW 21:22

But another important aspect of asking for what you want in life is the *way* you ask and the perseverance you put into that asking. You shouldn't think that asking for something just once will be sufficient – in fact, it will have almost no effect. Asking only once may work when you sit at the table with your family and ask one of them to pass you the bottle of water that's standing just out of reach, but asking the universe and the master is a totally different story.

When I look at Skottï from a master's perspective, I note that whenever he wants something he'll bark more than once. In reality, he could bark for a very long time before he gets something out of me. It's the same for us. Once more, nature works in the same way, whether you're a dog or a human being. Repetition is key in this exercise!

For Skottï, asking is still basic, and I guess a straight 'Woof, Woof ' is all that he needs, but he has to repeat it many times. For us human beings, I guess the main way to ask the universe or the master for something is through what we universally call a prayer. According to the dictionary, a prayer is 'a solemn request for help, or an expression of thanks addressed to God or another deity'.

When we say a prayer and repeat it day and night, we're doing what Skottï does when he asks for a bone that's beyond his reach! It's the same for everyone. Sometimes, Skottï has to repeat his prayer – Woof, Woof – hundreds of times over before the master obliges.

But there's also another catch here: sometimes Skottï can bark as much as he wants, but I may not comply with his wish. For instance, if I know that he's already had too much food, barking for another piece of chicken is futile.

Whenever I open the fridge, Skottï is not too far away and always comes by in the hope of being given something to eat. If I fetch a piece of chocolate, Skottï will wait to see if he'll get his share. However, because I know that chocolate isn't good for dogs, there's no way that will happen.

As I've explained, as his master, I'll only do what's in Skotti's best interest. This principle also applies to us with our own master and the higher power. The law of nature is the same for everyone – dogs and humans alike! But how does this operate at our level? We know now that the universe is abundant. In fact, the universe is just like a huge fridge full of many different and delicious treats that we can dream of. (This fridge is naturally much bigger than my own, as I'm just a human master of a small dog!)

But, at our level, this also means that we may not always get what we want, even if we ask for it. It's the same as it is for Skottï: whatever's in the fridge of the universe is not necessarily meant for us. It's a world of abundance but will we get the chocolate if it's bad for us? No!

As a matter of fact, it's not up to us to decide if we can have what we want. It's up to the master, as he/she is looking after us in the best way possible and works on a larger scale. He/she takes into account many other parameters that we may not even be aware of at that moment.

Let's not forget that the universe, the master, or the energy of life, works for *everyone* at the same time, not for one single individual. It has no particular reason to answer one person's prayer or wish over another's. Everything is connected in the end and the universe keeps everything in place and tries its best to make everybody happy. Its main intention is to deliver for the highest good of all, and not just one.

You might not always get what you want. But you'll certainly get what you need. That's the principle. The master is there to decide for you. More than anybody else, the master knows best, and you should always remind yourself of this principle.

In cases of frustration or doubt, we need to go back to the first principle and just trust and have faith in the master. Everything happens for the best (and for everybody's best), and whatever is going on in our life is exactly what we need at that point (even if it doesn't look like it).

If you're not happy with this – which is normal, at times – I suggest you revisit (as I regularly do) the third principle about gratitude. This will help you cope during hard times. If you're not getting what you want yet, start trying to be grateful for what you already have!

~

Chapter 5

Practise unconditional love

In the introduction to this book, I said that if there's one thing all dog owners would certainly agree on, it's the idea that their dog loves them unconditionally. In fact, that's one of the main reasons dogs are so popular and have been called 'man's best friend' for centuries. We all have a fair idea of what love is and how to express it, but nevertheless, *unconditional* love is something different.

When I consider Skottï's love for me, it's fair to say that I see it as unconditional. (Unconditional meaning, 'no matter what'.) He wags his tail whenever he sees me, no matter what kind of mood I'm in. If he breaks something accidentally, and is yelled at for it, he'll still come back and be ready with a big wet kiss. He can forgive and forget instantly, regardless of how either of us behaves.

However, as much as we appreciate the unconditional love we receive from our favourite pet, it's still very challenging to practise unconditional love with human beings. That's because our ego will come into the picture. For example, you can certainly say that you love your best friend, but does that really mean that your love is unconditional? Let's be honest, when we love a person, we almost always expect something in return: 'I love you, but only if you love me back.'

A dog's unconditional love sets a benchmark and I believe that one breed in particular sets the bar even higher. In Spain, the Spanish greyhound, or *galgo*, is used to hunt hares in the countryside as it's the fastest dog breed, reaching a maximum speed of around 60kph (37mph). There are around 190,000 hunters in Spain using *galgos* in this way, generally during the winter months, but what's not so widely known is the terrible treatment these dogs receive from their owners.

It starts with the animals' training to become the best hunters. In order to build endurance, some are attached to pickup trucks and forced to run for more than 20km (12 miles). Once the *galgos* get old or fail to perform well enough – which generally happens after around three to four years of hunting – they are destroyed in a variety of inhumane ways or abandoned by their owners, sometimes tied to a tree in a faraway wood. In Spain, it's definitely not good to be born a hare or a greyhound.

It's said that when a hunter ties a *galgo* to a tree in the woods, he also breaks both its front legs, as one broken leg would enable the dog to find its way back to its owner – if, by chance, it managed to unhook itself from the tree. You can't get a better example of unconditional love than that! It's estimated that there are 50,000 *galgos* killed or abandoned every year in Spain; the luckier ones are adopted in neighbouring countries.

While reading the excellent *Manifest Your Destiny* by Dr Wayne W. Dyer, I came across a passage from the New Testament that he'd used as a definition of love; I really liked it, and have shared it below:

> *'Love is patient, love is kind. It does not envy, it does not boast, it is not proud. It is not rude, it is not self-seeking, it is not easily angered, it keeps*

no record of wrongs. Love does not delight in evil but rejoices with the truth. It always protects, always trusts, always hopes, always perseveres.'

1 CORINTHIANS 13 4–7

As I read those words, I could think only of Skottï. I could easily replace the word 'love' with 'Skottï' without changing the text's meaning. This was leading to an obvious conclusion: love is equal to Skottï or Skottï is equal to love! Doing the same exercise with my own name didn't sound the same and that showed me I still have work to do in this area. I suggest you do the same exercise and see how it sounds.

The unconditional love, or love without condition, that Skottï displays so easily is definitely not easy for us to reach. However, it's something that we should try to practise as often as possible. You mainly need to get rid of your ego's domination over what you do and say, which seems to be the main blockage to reaching this state.

But the result will be worth the effort. The most important thing you'll gain from cultivating unconditional love is freedom from hate and violence. These will be replaced by joy and peace. You'll also be freed from the ego and from self-importance.

At this point in the book, it may be best to try to recall the first four principles and attempt to assimilate them. Another good idea would be to put the book aside and go for an outing, which leads us to the next principle.

~

Chapter 6

Play
with nature

Skottï loves his morning walk. Every day, my wife takes him to the seafront for a good hour. There he can run at will and interact with others dogs that are perhaps gurus-to-be. He loves to stand on the parapet and just watch the birds flying by, feel the breeze from the sea and catch the first rays of the sun. He's a good runner and always tries his luck on the black crows who, like him, enjoy this moment of freedom in the open.

If for any reason this daily outing doesn't happen, as you can imagine, Skottï's mood changes for the worse. He seems to become a bit sad and his eyes lose their sparkle – there's clearly a need in him that isn't being met.

I think this is an obvious call to tell us that we need to keep in touch with nature on a regular basis. If it works for Skottï, it should work for us! If a lack of interaction with natural elements such as the wind, the air and the sun has an effect on a dog, there's no reason why that shouldn't be the case for us, too.

Being outdoors opens up your mind and spirit to all kinds of new ideas and creativity. It offers a much-needed break from the 24/7 work environment. As we learned earlier, everything is connected, and it's important to feel and understand the vibration that emanates from us. This vibration is not constant and it needs to be revived – much like a rechargeable battery.

This is why being outside is so important: it allows us to get back in tune with the natural vibration of nature and the universe; it enables us to absorb this energy and transform it internally.

Once you start relating to nature, it'll bring you the mental oxygen you need. Moreover, being in touch with nature, and taking time sometimes to rediscover it, can bring you a different kind of internal peace.

Once we realize how intricate nature is, that everything is linked and how much beauty can be seen in a flower, a tree or the birds, we start to understand that there *has* to be some form of real power that drives everything for the better.

Understanding this, and adopting it as a personal philosophy, allows us to surrender to life itself and just *know* that everything is perfect, exactly the way it is. Everything always happens for the best.

The more you trust in the wisdom that creates all, the more you'll trust in yourself. The result of this trust is that an enormous sense of peace becomes available to you. This removes any internal questioning and brings peace of mind to the way you lead your life; even if nothing is perfect in that moment, it actually *is*!

Being at peace with yourself is a big achievement that can dramatically improve your daily life. For those living in congested and overcrowded cities, it may not be possible to dedicate time to nature every day – but hey, nature doesn't have to be grand. We don't need a 5-km (3-mile) stretch of seafront or a huge forest for a simple walk.

You can reconnect with nature by going into your garden or visiting a local park where you can sit and simply observe your surroundings. No garden? Maybe you have a balcony? What about growing baby tomatoes or your favourite flowers there? Gardening, in any form, has been found to calm the soul, and it's productive too!

While you're reconnecting with nature, or starting to get in touch with the elements, it's also very important to breathe deeply and stay in the now – a practice you learned in the second principle.

~

Chapter 7

Improve the way you relate to others

S kottï is a very social dog: he loves it when we have visitors and always greets them by jumping into the air with great enthusiasm. Those who are used to this find it adorable and those who are unfamiliar with dogs seem to get a little overwhelmed by it.

Besides human beings, Skottï also loves to meet other dogs. Whenever he goes for his walk, he looks out for others of his kind and greets them by going closer to wherever they are. Dogs have this routine, which is surprising to us, where they need to sniff each other's behind just to say 'hello'.

But the interesting thing in all this is that Skottï and all the other dogs interact happily with one another without any kind of discrimination. Be it a smaller dog, a bigger dog, a male, a female, long hair, short hair, dirty (by human standards), clean, black fur or white fur… the list could go on – none of these things matter to them!

You can see that the way dogs connect is simply by means of pure love and compassion. There's no jealousy involved – a small dog wouldn't greet a bigger one feeling insecure and inferior because of its height. And dogs don't hold grudges: they are never mean to each other if things don't go their way.

Isn't this great? Can you imagine how life would be if we humans did the same: meeting and talking to others without labelling or judging them like we always do. You can clearly see that there's no ego involved in this process, which is mostly what makes it happen. Humans are far too driven by the ego to display the same behaviour.

Of course, the idea of this principle is not to start speaking to *everyone* you meet when you're out and about. If you live in a mega city like Mumbai, Paris or New York, that exercise would certainly be interesting! I doubt anyone would reach their destination if they had to interact, even if just for two minutes, with everyone they met.

Nevertheless, the message here is to open up to others more than you're used to doing and try to keep the pace as much as possible. At least, that's what dog owners do when they meet other dog owners during their daily outings. Pushed and pulled by their pets to go meet other dogs, at some point the humans have no choice other than to speak to each other. Often, those people wouldn't have spoken to anyone if they'd been alone without their dog to break the ice and enable them to start a conversation.

The idea is also to accept 'the other' more easily and not be prejudiced or hold grudges. Humans are probably the only species that are able to hold a grudge. No dog will ever be angry with you because you didn't give him a treat after dinner. Holding a grudge weighs you down emotionally and keeps you from moving forward in your life. So, let grudges go, along with all kinds of judgment against 'the other'.

We should always remember that we're all the same – breathing the same air, living on the same Earth. The colour of our skin, the language we speak or the community we belong to, are not important. At the end of the day, all humans, even if they look different from the outside, encounter the same feelings.

We all have that in common, and we all know what it's like to feel love and happiness, but also fear or guilt. Whatever feelings you've experienced, you can be sure that you're not alone and that someone has already felt the same way.

The other lesson I learned from Skottï and the way he interacts with his friends is that we should accept ourselves the way we are. Skottï has no issues around self-acceptance – I can't imagine him wishing he were a German shepherd so he could run faster and jump higher.

We humans tend to spend a lot of time comparing ourselves with others and trying to make ourselves look like someone else instead of loving our unique features, our unique life and also our unique problems. As this popular saying rightly states: 'Be yourself. Everyone else is already taken!'

~

Chapter 8

Be patient

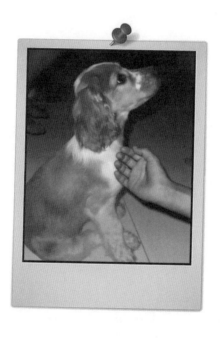

I've always been amazed by Skottï's ability to simply wait patiently for his master to return home. The best part is that the longer the wait, the more happiness he shows! If this is the rule of nature, it means that the more you wait, the higher the reward will be.

In the past, I found being patient a struggle. While job-hunting, I'd expect to get a call immediately after the interview, but with some companies, the recruitment process can be much longer. If I got stuck in traffic and missed a green light, I'd get very upset, blaming the car in front for not going faster at the intersection.

That was until I started spending quality time with Skottï and realized that being impatient was a losing battle that didn't help anyone. My guru was right in front of me and he offered an example of how to deal with the situation.

I finally understood that time is a constraint that isn't always within our control. In nature, everything takes the time it *needs*. Look at a flower: from the seed to the bud about to bloom, there's a full cycle that needs to take place, step by step, invariably.

Will it help to water the flower more often, hoping that more food will accelerate the process? Or to just pull the stem? Will it help to dig in the soil to check whether the process has started or if the seed has just popped out? Not really. In fact, doing any of those things would almost certainly be counterproductive. Nature follows its own path at its own rhythm and this needs to be respected.

Skottï knows it all — his master will come in due time and there's no need to bark for it to happen sooner. Whenever we hope for something to happen, it follows the same logic. If we agree to say that the universe does its best to achieve it, the universe also needs its own time to do the same. And it needs to work it out in accordance with all the different parameters, of which we may not be aware.

It may take time for what we want to be delivered to us. In fact, it will be delivered to us at the exact required time. This is certainly a small principle for a better life, but it's a very strong one, as it can release a lot of unnecessary stress.

The importance of patience is underlined in this passage from the Bible:

> *'Be patient, therefore, brothers, until the coming of the Lord. See how the farmer waits for the precious fruit of the earth, being patient about it, until it receives the early and the late rains.'*
>
> JAMES 5:7

In the end, just bear in mind that patience is a virtue that you learn with patience.

Chapter 9

Use your intuition

In May 2015, my family decided to visit me in Delhi where I was then based – the city was supposed to be the base camp for our summer holiday that year.

While I'm in Delhi, I love going to the forest next to Qutub Minar, the famous minaret that stands tall and proud in the southern part of the city. In India's heavily polluted capital, the forest seems like an oasis in a desert: it's full of deer and peacocks and I'd often come across many foxes, especially in the winter when I'd bicycle in the early hours of the morning.

On the morning of 12 May, I took Skottï for a long walk in the forest. He always enjoyed it there because he could momentarily escape his city-dweller life and run in the wild, but that morning his behaviour was odd. He was rather agitated and began running in circles and barking for no apparent reason. I tried to spot the usual deer and peacocks but there were none.

Once we'd returned home, I learned from my family and neighbours that there had been an earthquake. Its epicentre had been somewhere in North India, but because it had measured 7.3 on the Richter scale, it had been strong enough to violently shake the windows and doors in our home.

Out in the forest, I hadn't noticed the effects of the earthquake but Skotti certainly had, hence the change in his behaviour. Dogs and other animals have an ability to sense such an occurrence. We can call it a sixth sense or an instinct they have and are able to listen to.

It's very interesting to know that this instinct exists in the animal kingdom, and there's no reason why human beings would have been spared this faculty. In fact, as creatures of the universe, we too have instinct running inside us, but, unfortunately, we don't really know about it, or perhaps more accurately, we've forgotten it exists.

It starts from the moment we're born. For no reason other than instinct, a newborn baby will always take its first breath. This is natural and simply part of the miracle of life. Moreover, all newborn babies are put through a range of medical tests by nurses and/or paediatricians, just minutes after they are born, to assess their general health.

Many of these health checks are designed to test the reflexes and instinctive behaviours that are rooted within all human beings. The primitive stepping test checks the walking reflex. A healthy baby will make a walking motion when held up with one hand across its chest.

Another is the protective reflex test in which a soft cloth is placed over the baby's eyes and nose. The baby will instinctively arch her/his head, turn it side-to-side and bring both hands toward the face to move the cloth away.

Then comes the rooting reflex test in which the newborn turns his or her head to find the breast when touched on either side of the cheek. Automatically and very naturally, the baby will start the sucking mechanism.

The result of these tests suggest that because we have these natural instincts and energies that push us toward life at birth, there's no reason why they wouldn't exist at the adult stage. Between birth and adulthood many things happen that fundamentally change us, but the main thing is the development of consciousness and the process of thinking — which are not there at the very beginning of our life.

Our intellectual mind, ruled by logic and rational thoughts gained from our own experiences in life, takes over our entire thinking process, forcing instinct and intuition to take a backseat.

That's the main difference between dogs and us. We often say that having a dog at home is like having a three- or four-year-old toddler. That's the age when a child's intellectual faculties really start developing, and when their intellectual mind broadens and gains importance.

This doesn't mean that our built-in instinct — which is part of our subconscious — is no longer active, it's just that now our mind is too loud in comparison with the small voice of the instinct. We simply lose touch with it, as well as our ability to trust. Nevertheless, we should know that this instinct, intuition or sixth sense is always within us – we just need to find a way to listen to it.

Sometimes we experience it unknowingly. For instance, it can happen when you first meet someone and just by shaking their hand you feel that this acquaintance may not be the best for you. Love at first sight is another example of our intuition shouting to us that we have a strong connection with the person we've just met.

Imagine entering a room and sensing that the people in it might have been involved in a big fight or argument beforehand. When this happens it's because you are able to *feel* the negative vibe in the air.

Intuition has several purposes and mainly works to:

- Warn you of danger.

- Connect you with others and enlighten you on their thoughts and feelings.

- Illuminate the mind with insight and inspiration.

- Take control of thinking during a crisis (when the survival instinct clearly takes over).

The interesting thing about intuition or the sixth sense is that, normally, it communicates through the physical senses, or feelings that can be recognized if you notice the way you react to certain situations from your own experiences.

So, just by listening to your body, you'll already have some idea of what's going on and thus find guidance in the right direction. When this happens you need to try to quieten the mind, as the intellectual or logical aspects of it will always tend to ignore those signs.

In fact, we need to recall the animal that's hidden within us – to still the mind and listen to the body: see how it feels, how it reacts. You may get goose bumps, or your heart may start to beat faster; you may experience sweating, vertigo or stomach ache. On the other hand, you could experience the sensation of plenitude in your heart and what can be described as 'your heart being at peace'.

I like the advice given by Eckhart Tolle in his book, *The Power of Now*. According to him, if there's an apparent conflict between what you think about something and what your overall physical feeling about it is, you should follow what your body is saying, as the thought on the particular matter will be a lie and the feeling or emotion will be the truth.

Once again, it shows that intuition or instinct is much stronger than the mind, whose thoughts are driven by different parameters that can have a big influence.

Here are some other interesting quotes on the subject of intuition:

> *'Built into you is an internal guidance system that shows you the way home. All you need to do is heed the voice.'*
>
> NEALE DONALD WALSCH

> *'It is through science that we prove, but through intuition that we discover.'*
>
> HENRI POINCARÉ

> *'The intuitive mind is a sacred gift and the rational mind is a faithful servant. We have created a society that honours the servant and has forgotten the gift.'*
>
> ALBERT EINSTEIN

Chapter 10

Beware of Pavlovian conditioning

Many of you will have heard of the Russian scientist and physiologist Ivan Pavlov who, at the beginning of the 20th century, conducted experiments that revealed that dogs react to certain stimuli that trigger their behaviour. His discovery was later named Pavlovian conditioning.

Pavlov began his work with the idea that there are some things that dogs don't need to learn. For example, they don't need to learn to salivate whenever they see food. This comes naturally to them as a reflex that's built into their system. It's known as an unconditioned response.

Pavlov highlighted the existence of the unconditioned response by presenting a dog with some food and measuring its salivary secretions. Nevertheless, he also discovered, somewhat accidently, that the dog would also start salivating when the lab assistant entered the room without any food to offer. Basically, any object or event that a dog learned to associate with food would trigger the same response.

This was a learned behaviour because, at the beginning of the experiment, Pavlov's dogs didn't do it and there was a point when they started. Their behaviour had changed and a change in behaviour of this type must be the result of learning.

Pavlov continued his experiments by using a bell as his stimulus. Whenever he gave food to his dogs he also rang a bell. After the procedure was repeated a number of times the dogs started salivating whenever the bell was rung, even when no food was given. So we can say that the dogs created and learned an association between the bell and the food, and that a new behaviour had been learned. We say that there was a conditioned response due to the stimulus.

If you have a dog and have tried to teach him tricks, you'll certainly have used the same procedure. For instance, if you've been trying to teach your dog to sit, and as part of the training routine offered him his favourite snack, it won't have taken long for him to sit whenever you ask him to, since he'll be hoping for the snack that was given when the training started.

In his brain, a connection is created between the act of sitting and getting a treat. Even after time passes, when you give him the command to sit, neurons in his brain will send a signal that reminds him that if he does as he's told, he'll receive something good to eat.

It's not because of conscious memory that the dog will execute the command in exchange for a treat, but because of the way his brain has been wired during the training period. This behaviour has now been rooted within the dog as a routine.

You might be wondering how this affects *us*. Well, if we agree that there's an animal in every human – or that there's an animal side to us – there's nothing wrong in looking at the 'animal' part of us. We can say fairly that human beings are animals with something extra, which is consciousness. So, if we put aside consciousness for one moment, there isn't much difference between us and our dogs.

As a result, I think it's fair to say that our 'animal side' can also, just like dogs, be affected at some level by Pavlovian conditioning, or some routines. Our conditioning works in the same way as for dogs – mainly through excessive repetition.

As the author don Miguel Ruiz so nicely formulated in his books: human beings are domesticated animals. The education process starts the minute we are born, as certain beliefs driven by the people with whom we interact most often get built into our system.

Naturally, it starts with our immediate and extended family, and is followed by the school education system and the peer groups we form. There's also the influence of the community, religion or ethnic group we belong to. All these factor play a big role in the way our mind is formatted and, ultimately, how we'll respond to any event in our life.

It's a natural process and, as a child, we're driven by it without realizing its power. At the end of the day, for most of us, our beliefs are the same as those of our parents. We look at the world through lenses that were shaped from the very start, without realizing that we could see the world through our very own eyes.

Repeatedly, the way we think, the way we act and our morals and rules, become our own routine. This determines our behaviour in many situations, as demonstrated in the following story.

In India, where we've been living for many years now, it's still very common to have household goods delivered to your doorstep. Thus, throughout the day, there are several people coming and going through our door to deliver the milk, newspaper, groceries, etc. This is certainly very exciting for Skottï, who is always happy to greet newcomers at home, but I did notice that the boys' reaction to him differed. Let's delve deeper…

Whenever a delivery boy arrived, Skottï would naturally bark and, in his excitement, head towards him for his typical welcome dance, tuned to the rhythm of his tail. He would also try to smell the boy, since that's his way of recognizing people.

The fact that people react differently to the same situation stems from the beliefs that were engraved in their minds during childhood. I finally understood that, in general, the delivery boys who were *not* happy to meet Skottï were Muslim.

Now, before anyone pounces on me for discrimination, let me explain that this was directly linked to their religious beliefs. I discovered that the main reason some Muslims don't like dogs stems from a particular theological teaching they receive, which is that angels are afraid of dogs (this is according to what Muhammad said).

I also came to understand that, for Muslims, black dogs are even considered demonic. Luckily, Skottï is a light brown colour, so I hope coming to our place wasn't too dramatic for them! The delivery boys always got a good tip, so hopefully that made up for the unsolicited encounter with our dog.

In any event, this is a perfect example of mental conditioning and the direct effect it has on the way we happen to live our lives. It's important to remember that, as humans, we have the ability to simply put aside our consciousness in certain situations.

Yes, this consciousness of ours is an important tool that offers us the possibility of stepping back and analyzing our own behaviour and what's happening in our lives, but it's important to mention that this requires a lot of personal effort from within. That's why I said that consciousness 'offers us the *possibility*' of doing this exercise. It's not automatic for us to do it. We have a powerful tool but it's up to us whether or not we use it.

Many of us will just live our lives without really questioning ourselves and, convinced that we're always right, will never think of challenging ourselves, but others will open up and understand the process. I believe that, in reading this book, you're in the category of people who are always eager to learn and who know that personal development is a continuous process.

You may not necessarily be the same person you were a few years ago. You can perhaps accept that your ideas can change over time and that what you believed was right at some point in your life may not be so right anymore. You know how to use your consciousness and intelligence to your benefit. You're able to step back, look at your life without judgment and admit that, in some way, you may have been influenced by your own inbuilt routines.

Albert Einstein said that, 'We cannot solve our problems with the same thinking we used when we created them.' We clearly understand that something has to change if we want the outcome to be different, which leads us to more of Einstein's wisdom: 'Change your thinking and you change your life.'

~

Chapter 11

Do yoga:
the dog poses

After taking inspiration from Skottï in terms of the way he carries on with his life, I also thought it would be beneficial to physically act like him as well. The idea wasn't to start barking and galloping on four legs but to introduce some yoga poses into my life.

I'd heard about the benefits of yoga but never really tried it. Until one day I happened to read a book on the subject and became intrigued by the names given to all the different asanas (poses). I was very amused to discover that some of them had been named after dogs.

Watching my dear Skottï as he performed some of the asanas I'd seen in that book convinced me that yoga was worth trying. After all, Skottï had become my guru, so it was only natural for me to do what he was doing. Moreover, I happened to have periodic lower back pain and thought that perhaps yoga could be the solution.

I was very happy with the outcome and can only recommend everyone to dedicate some regular time to yoga. It has the ability to transform your life. Of course, it takes more than a few sessions to become good at it but, like everything, one needs to start.

There are many different yoga poses but you don't need to do all of them to see the benefits. I can certainly recommend the two postures that take their name from our guru. The first of these is the 'Downward-Facing Dog' pose. This is named after the way dogs naturally stretch their entire bodies.

It's one of the most recognized yoga poses and can be practised by beginners. It can be used as a transitional pose, a resting pose and a strength-builder, and really should form part of your daily yoga session.

Downward-Facing Dog is beneficial in numerous ways. It energizes and rejuvenates the entire body, and deeply stretches the hamstrings, shoulders, calves, arches, hands and spine, while building strength in the arms, shoulders and legs. It also lengthens the spine and strengthens the muscles of the chest, increasing lung capacity.

In this position the heart is higher than the head so circulation to the brain is increased. This, in turn, brings benefits such as relief from headaches, insomnia, fatigue and mild depression. The flow of blood to the brain also calms the nervous system, improves memory and concentration, and relieves stress.

It's said that regularly practising Downward-Facing Dog pose can improve digestion, relieve back pain and help prevent osteoporosis. It's also known to be therapeutic for sinusitis, asthma and flat feet. Phew!

Given its many benefits, I can now understand why all dogs seem to naturally do this pose on a regular basis. Nevertheless, it's not recommended for people who suffer from high blood pressure, weak eye capillaries or shoulder injuries. Moreover, it's much better to learn yoga postures while under the supervision of a trained practitioner. Having said that, for those of you who have never done yoga and want to get a quick feel for this position, simply follow these steps:

Downward-Facing Dog

1. On a mat, get onto all fours. Form a table position, with your back as the tabletop and your arms and upper legs as the table legs. Align the wrists directly beneath the shoulders and the knees directly under the hips.

2. As you exhale, lift up the hips and gently begin to straighten the legs. Make sure you don't lock the knees but form an inverted V-shape with the body. Imagine that the hips and thighs are being pulled backward from the top of the thighs.

3. The hands are shoulder-width apart, the feet are hip-width apart and parallel to each other, and the toes point straight ahead.

4. Press the hands into the ground as you lift through the pelvis. Widen through the shoulder blades. Keep the neck lengthened by touching the ears to the inner arms. As you lengthen the spine, lift the hip bones up toward the ceiling. Now, press down equally through the heels and

the palms of the hands. The heels may or may not touch the floor, depending on the flexibility of the lower back, hamstrings and calf muscles. The more you practise, the easier it will be to get your heels to the floor.

5. Hold the Downward Dog pose for between five and 20 long, deep breaths. Look toward the navel as you do so.

6. To release, exhale as you gently bend the knees and return to table position. Relax.

Then we come to the 'Upward-Facing Dog'. This is a backbend pose that stretches the back, providing relief from lower back pain. It can be used as a strength-builder and also as a step toward deeper backbends.

It stretches the chest and spine, while at the same time strengthening the wrists, arms and shoulders. By strengthening and opening the upper body and chest, it improves posture and can be therapeutic for asthma. It also helps create suppleness in the back of the torso and abdomen, which stimulates the abdominal organs and improves digestion. Finally, it firms the buttocks and thighs, helping to relieve sciatica.

The backbend position energizes and rejuvenates the entire body, providing relief from fatigue and mild depression. Here are the steps for it:

Upward-Facing Dog

1. Begin by lying face down on a mat with the legs extended behind you, spread a few centimetres apart. The arms should be stretched down the length of the body. Do not tuck in your toes, as this can scrunch the spine.

2. Place the hands on the floor alongside the body, next to the lower ribs. Point the fingers toward the top of the mat and hug the elbows in, close to the ribcage.

3. As you inhale, press the palms firmly on the mat and straighten the arms, slowly lifting the torso, hips and knees a few centimetres off the mat. The entire weight of the body should be resting on the palms and the top of the feet.

4. Keep the elbows pressed alongside the body. Drop the shoulders away from the ears and lift the chest toward the ceiling.

5. You may look straight ahead or tilt the head slightly backward toward the ceiling, if your neck is sufficiently flexible.

6. Ensure that the wrists are in line with the shoulders and the neck is not strained.

7. Hold the pose for up to 30 seconds, taking deep breaths.

8. To release, exhale as you slowly lower the knees, hips and torso back onto the mat.

The more you practise yoga, the more the principles outlined in this book will become clear in your mind and start to make sense. Earlier, we talked about living in the now. I have learned that besides the physical dimension, there's also a mental, emotional and spiritual dimension to yoga.

Practising yoga is, in fact, all about being in the present moment – listening to your breath, watching your body and allowing them to work together during the different poses. Yoga always fixes you in the present moment. In time, you can learn to respond to the moments of your life with all your attention and energy, and replicate what's done during your yoga practice.

Yoga is also a good way to instil unconditional self-love. It teaches you to accept your limitations and be patient with yourself. Sometimes a pose will require months, if not years, of practice to be expressed to the utmost of your own potential. When you start doing yoga, you start your own inward journey. During this journey there will be a lot of self-discovery and self-acceptance.

You'll come to depend less and less on an outside source for your supply of happiness and love. There may be some poses with which you are uncomfortable on the first attempt. You'll come to understand that there's no point in trying harder – you just need to surrender, do your best, and develop a more compassionate relationship with yourself. Eventually, the pose will come to you – when your body is ready.

You'll understand that, in the end, all we need to do is trust the process of life. There is always a sense of magic to trust. Have faith, don't try to be in control, but truly surrender.

~

Conclusion

We've reached the end of the book but let's take one last lesson from the dog fraternity.

When a dog goes for a trip in his master's car, he's clearly unaware of the destination, yet he always enjoys the ride, sticking his head out of the window and feeling the breeze on his fur. Whether it's a day out or a trip to the vet for an unpleasant check-up or injection, it doesn't matter to the dog at the time of the ride. He doesn't even know how the car functions.

And this is the essential point: it's the journey that matters the most. If the car has to stop along the way, to fill up on petrol or to fix a flat tyre, you'll only see the driver looking hassled. To the dog, the delay doesn't matter.

In the same way, we should always take life as it comes and not get frustrated if things don't turn out the way we think they should. Let's not think too much about where we're heading. Let's avoid having too many expectations, and always believe that the master or the universe is looking after us and will only take us wherever we need to go for our highest benefit. Let's just put our head out of the window of life and feel the wind!

On a personal level, I now like to think that if I get an unexpected mechanical problem with my motorbike on the road, there must be a good reason for it, even if it delays me. I prefer to take it positively and believe that it may have occurred to save me from a more serious problem such as an accident somewhere up ahead.

It is said that motivation doesn't last, which is why we compare it to bathing — something we need to do every day. I cannot agree more with this. As we all know, staying positive and happy 24/7 is impossible. There's always something or other coming our way to spoil our mood. This is surely one of the reasons why motivational books sell like hot cakes nowadays.

For those of you who have a dog, I strongly suggest that whenever you feel a bit low, you stop whatever you're doing for just one minute, take a few deep breaths and simply look at your dog. He'll act as your vitamin, and by recalling all the principles outlined in this book, you can turn your mood around in seconds.

For those of you who don't have a dog, perhaps you're now tempted to get your very own four-legged companion! You'll never regret the decision. As you now know, a dog is more than a dog – it's like having a guru to remind you of how to live a good life.

It's unfortunate that dogs don't talk. They are so expressive in their own way that I always wonder what they would tell us if only they could speak. Skottï, being my guru, would certainly come up with a few good quotes, don't you think?

In his book *Discourse on the Method* (1637), the French philosopher René Descartes coined the Latin term *Cogito, ergo sum* (in English: 'I think, therefore I am'). This refers to the thinking identity of a human being as a self and, as a consequence, the proof that both 'I' and 'we' exist. However, we could then discuss what the 'I' we're referring to actually *is*? There's so much behind the 'I' – so many ideas, perceptions and images – that it is very difficult, when we are asked to describe who we are, to define ourselves in simple terms.

The thinking 'I' certainly originates from the mind and, as we've seen, doesn't necessarily translate into happiness in everyday life. In contrast, we can say that Skottï doesn't think, which, as per the Descartes principle, would mean that 'he's not', as in 'I do not think, therefore I am not'!

I'm far from being a philosopher but I certainly like playing with words and I amuse myself with many thoughts about the nature of 'I am'. I have to conclude that if Skottï *doesn't* think, he at least knows how to live a good and happy life, as we've seen throughout this book.

If Guru Skottï *could* speak – and therefore have the last word in this book – I presume he would say: 'I don't think much, therefore I'm happy'.

On this light note, I wish all readers a very happy life!

Acknowledgements

The year 2015 was not such an easy year. First, the loss of a job which took me by surprise and then, just one month later, I was flying back to Paris to be with my dad and family and bid farewell to my mum, who had passed away in her sleep after a long disease. Of course, mum had to go one day, like everyone, and there will always be another job, but it's at times like this that you start questioning everything. Why this? Why now?

I tried to find answers in all the self-help books I started reading at that time and I would first like to thank all those authors. They helped me to pass this period of my life and understand that everything always happen for a reason and everything always happen for the best.

It is now clear that this book was meant to be written now and may not have happened if 2015 had been different for me. So I guess I should just thank life for that.

I would also like to thank everyone who helped me in this project, which started as a personal challenge.

Thank you Skottï, who has been a very dear companion, always sitting nearby as I wrote and always happy to play whenever inspiration was lacking.

Thank you to the family, friends and acquaintances who gave me encouragement whenever I discussed the project with them.

Finally, I'd like to express my gratitude to my publisher, Hay House.

Firstly, Hay House India for their kind support and trust as they were very quick to believe in this book after reading only the first few chapters. After submitting the manuscript, I didn't expect a reply for months, so I was happily surprised when I received positive feedback and a publishing agreement just a few days later.

Also Hay House UK and its wonderful team who decided very quickly to give the book some international exposure and take it to places I could not have even dreamt about when I started the project.

And, needless to say, I'd like to thank the angels, wherever they are.